## THE *Missing* SHOP MANUAL

# BENCH PLANES

{ the tool information you need at your fingertips }

skills institute press

*Distributed By*
*Fox Chapel Publishing*

# FOX CHAPEL
PUBLISHING

# Contents

## Inside the Booklet

## On the DVD

*Introduction*

*When to use jointer, jack, and smoothing planes*

*The physics of how planes cut*

*Working up rough-sawn boards with bench planes*

*True face and true edge*

*Metal planes are easier to use than wooden planes*

*Planing the second face parallel to the first face*

*Planing end grain*

*Infill or stuffed planes (Norris-style planes)*

*Stanley-Bailey planes*

*Bedrock planes*

*Sharpening planes*

*Shooting boards to make and use*

ISBN 978-1-56523-538-0

DVD © 2010 by Ernie Conover. All Rights Reserved.

Text and Illustrations © 2010 by Skills Institute Press

Published by Fox Chapel Publishing Inc., 800-457-9112,
www.foxchapelpublishing.com

**I have been enamored with hand planes since I was a boy.** My woodworking career started at mid-twentieth century when plane manufacture was at an abysmal low. To find good planes, one had to look to the planes of previous generations, so collecting was at first driven by need. I have often debated whether I liked collecting or using hand planes more—suffice it to say it is a dead heat.

Planes are anthropomorphic; naming the parts and conditions tells us this—heel, toe, cheeks, sole, mouth, throat, and choking, to name a few. Like pets, they are sweet or temperamental, and a few are born feral, never doing man's bidding at all. I certainly have some favorites that I would mourn the loss of.

Nothing tells more about workers of the past than their tools. A peek in an old toolbox tells us a man's trade and how well he plied it. Many of the tools in an eighteenth-or nineteenth-century toolbox were planes, because a house carpenter in 1800 would have had about 40 of them. The fun of collecting is that specialized trades, such as coach and spar makers, had highly specialized planes. Unfortunately, dealers are selling toolboxes piecemeal today because they can realize a higher price that way. This is sad because a workman's history is erased in the process. If you can afford it, buy the whole box. An excuse you could offer to your significant other is that I have charged you with this holiest of tasks.

This all brings me to the tenet that we never own planes, we are only stewards of them for our lifetime. It is our duty to house and protect them and keep them as near original condition as possible. That is not to say we don't use them, for use adds our bit of history. Old or new, just keep them in a dry cupboard or toolbox and don't paint them new colors. Ride them hard but don't put them away wet.

Museum conservators endeavor to do nothing invasive to items in their charge. All work and finishing is in the spirit of the original and would be reversible if future generations decided that our work was ill-advised. Some materials that will help you to be a good steward are paraffin, paste wax, and white shellac.

Crayoning paraffin on the soles of metal or wood planes greatly reduces friction, which means reduced wear. Paste wax on metal parts offers some rust protection. The underside of the cap irons of Stanley Bailey and Bedrock planes made up through the late 1920s had a blue finish left by the heat-treating process. Do not scrub this original finish away with abrasives. The best protection is a simple coat of white shellac, which will preserve the original finish and prevent rusting. If the cap iron is slightly rusted, the shellac will cut off air and prevent further rusting.

Starting in the 1930s, the lever caps of Stanley Bailey and Bedrock planes were nickel plated. Do not use abrasive on these surfaces or the finish will be destroyed. The best restorative is a good chrome polish. Once the metal has been polished, paste wax is the best protection. The black portions these planes were treated with an asphalt-based finish called *asphaltum*, but often referred to as *japanning*. It was a viscous material applied by dipping the metal part and then baking it at high temperature.

Japanning is a very tough finish that will hold up well. If spots are missing, even rusted away, do not sand-blast the plane body to clean and paint it. The best treatment is to wash the body in warm water and strong detergent and immediately dry it. Now brush on a coat of white shellac, which will brighten the japanning to near original and protect the bare metal from further rusting. The beauty of paraffin, paste wax, and white shellac is that they are all reversible. Alcohol will remove them all and do no harm to the japanning, nickel plate, or bare metal.

Above all, have fun with planes. Using them is Zen-like and aerobic at the same time. Plane that tabletop, and you can cancel your trip to the gym.

*Ernie Conover*

# A NOTE ABOUT THE DVD

One of my complaints about video is over-compression of events so as not to bore the viewer. You see a board fly through a machine with no mention of the setup to do this job. Any fool can run the board, but the setup is not so obvious. Important facts are often left out, to say the least. Therefore I have endeavored to show as much in real time as possible and only leave out important steps when they are repeated, such is when planing the second side of a plank. While dissolves are used to switch from camera to camera, no time is missing. Anytime we have decided to chop a bit out so as to not bore you to tears, we have used the convention of fade to black to denote missing time. — ERC

# PLANES

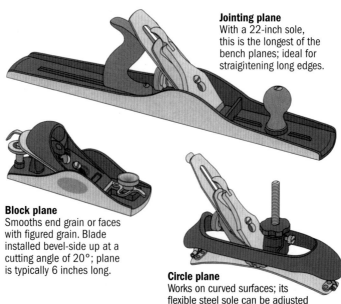

**Jointing plane**
With a 22-inch sole, this is the longest of the bench planes; ideal for straightening long edges.

**Block plane**
Smooths end grain or faces with figured grain. Blade installed bevel-side up at a cutting angle of 20°; plane is typically 6 inches long.

**Circle plane**
Works on curved surfaces; its flexible steel sole can be adjusted to conform to either concave or convex workpieces.

**Jack plane**
A general-purpose plane for smoothing rough boards and flattening uneven surfaces; available with a corrugated sole to reduce friction. Typically 14 inches long.

**Bullnose rabbet plane**
A snub-nosed, 4-inch-long version of the shoulder plane *(facing page)* for smoothing in tight places; its detachable nose makes it ideal for trimming stopped rabbets.

### Shoulder plane
Trims tenon shoulders square; sides are perfectly square with sole, enabling plane to cut with equal precision upright or on either side.

### Panel-raising plane
Its angled sole allows it to bevel panel edges; features a traditional wooden plane adjustment mechanism. Available with the iron skewed to the left or right so plane can always cut with the grain.

### Rabbet and filister plane
Cuts rabbets; can be used either with or against the grain. Features an adjustable guide fence and a depth stop as well as a steel spur for working against the grain; for trimming, use the forward blade position.

### Router plane
A specialty plane that routs out grooves and dados, and cleans out shallow mortises; features both chisel and pointed cutters, and an adjustable depth gauge.

### Bench rabbet plane
A larger—typically, 13-inch-long—version of the smoothing plane for cutting large rabbets; its blade extends across the entire width of the sole.

*Planes*

# ANATOMY OF A BENCH PLANE

## Steel-Bodied Smoothing Plane

Smooths faces and edges to prepare wood surfaces; typically 9½ inches long.

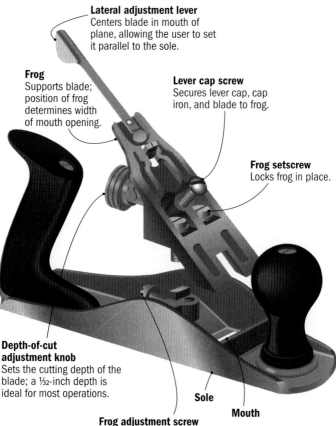

**Lateral adjustment lever**
Centers blade in mouth of plane, allowing the user to set it parallel to the sole.

**Frog**
Supports blade; position of frog determines width of mouth opening.

**Lever cap screw**
Secures lever cap, cap iron, and blade to frog.

**Frog setscrew**
Locks frog in place.

**Depth-of-cut adjustment knob**
Sets the cutting depth of the blade; a ½32-inch depth is ideal for most operations.

**Sole**

**Mouth**

**Frog adjustment screw**
Turned to slide frog back and forth, widening, or narrowing mouth opening; should be positioned so that opening is between ½32 and ½16 inch.

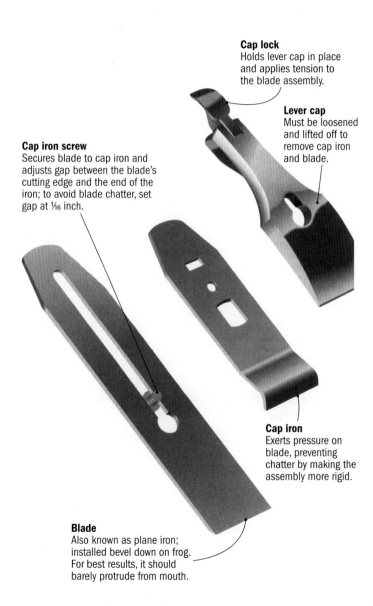

**Cap lock**
Holds lever cap in place and applies tension to the blade assembly.

**Lever cap**
Must be loosened and lifted off to remove cap iron and blade.

**Cap iron screw**
Secures blade to cap iron and adjusts gap between the blade's cutting edge and the end of the iron; to avoid blade chatter, set gap at ¹⁄₁₆ inch.

**Cap iron**
Exerts pressure on blade, preventing chatter by making the assembly more rigid.

**Blade**
Also known as plane iron; installed bevel down on frog. For best results, it should barely protrude from mouth.

# SETTING UP

A plane must be sharp and properly adjusted to shear off shavings of wood—often as thin as paper—with no tearout. Before using a new plane you will have to sharpen the blade and adjust the tool for top performance. The procedure involves two steps: creating a bevel on the blade's cutting edge and honing another bevel on part of the first one, called a microbevel; then removing, or "lapping," the burr that results from the honing process.

*A nicked or out-of-square plane blade can be salvaged by squaring its end on a grinder. The guide helps keep the blade perpendicular to the grinding wheel.*

If the cutting edge is damaged in any way, or if you are trying to restore an old blade, you first need to square its end. As shown in the photo at right, a grinder is the best tool to use for this purpose.

Whether you work with steel-bodied or wooden planes, setting them up requires very little in the way of specialized equipment. Honing can be accomplished with a combination sharpening stone and a commercial honing guide. Adjusting a plane's depth of cut requires only a screwdriver. The sole of a wooden plane becomes naturally slick with use; however, rubbing a little paraffin wax on the bottom of any plane will help to reduce friction.

Hone your blades frequently to maintain a keen edge and always retract them into the plane after use. Store the plane upright to prevent the sole from being harmed by other tools.

# HONING A PLANE BLADE

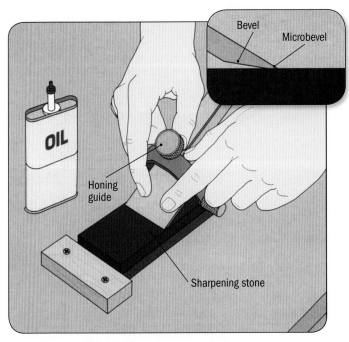

Bevel

Microbevel

Honing guide

Sharpening stone

## Creating a bevel and honing a microbevel

Place a combination sharpening stone coarse side up on a work surface. Nail cleats to the table against the stone to keep it from moving. Clamp the blade top face up in a commercial honing guide set for a 30° bevel. Saturate the stone with the appropriate lubricant—either water or a light oil—until it pools on the surface. Then, holding the honing guide, slide the blade back and forth from end to end along the stone *(above)*, grinding the bevel. To hone the microbevel, reposition the blade in the guide, raise the angle by 5°, and turn the stone over. Saturate the stone again and repeat the process, applying moderate pressure until a microbevel forms *(inset)*.

# HONING A PLANE BLADE *(continued)*

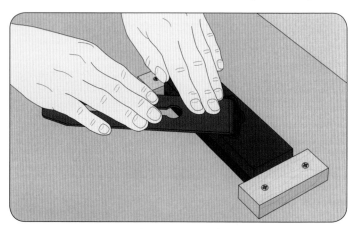

### Lapping the burr

To remove the burr—a thin ridge of metal that forms on the flat face of the blade as a result of honing the microbevel—remove the blade from the honing guide and saturate the fine side of the stone once again. Holding the blade perfectly flat on the stone, bevel side up *(above)*, move it in a circular pattern on the stone until the flat side of the cutting edge is smooth. Test the sharpness of the cutting edge on a piece of paper; a sharp blade will slice a sliver from the paper's edge.

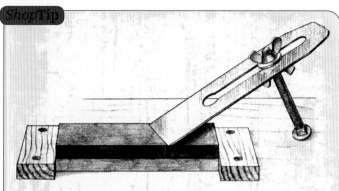

### A shop-made honing jig

If you do not own a commercial honing guide, you can still get good results sharpening plane blades using this simple jig. Slip a 4-inch-long, ⅜-inch-diameter carriage bolt through the blade's slot. Fasten with washers and wing nuts on both sides of the blade. With the blade on the sharpening stone and the head of the bolt on your work surface, use a protractor and a sliding bevel to adjust the wing nuts so that the blade can be slid along the stone at the proper angle.

# ADJUSTING A PLANE

## Positioning the blade assembly

Position the cap iron on the top face of the blade with the cutting edge of the blade extending about $\frac{1}{16}$ inch beyond the end of the cap iron. Tighten the cap iron screw *(right, top)*. Then place the blade assembly—including the blade, cap iron and lever cap—in position on the frog. The gap between the front edge of the blade and the front of the mouth should be between $\frac{1}{32}$ and $\frac{1}{16}$ inch. If the gap is too wide or narrow, remove the blade assembly and loosen both frog setscrews about $\frac{1}{4}$ turn. Then adjust the frog adjustment

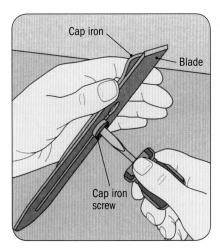

Cap iron

Blade

Cap iron screw

Frog adjustment screw

Frog setscrews

screw to set the proper gap *(right, bottom)*. Tighten the setscrews and reposition the blade assembly on the frog, locking it in place with the cap lock.

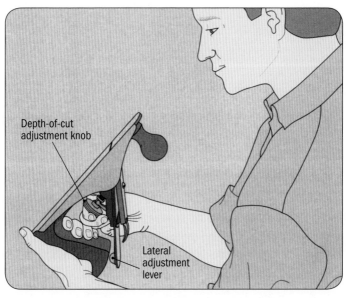

Depth-of-cut
adjustment knob

Lateral
adjustment
lever

## Centering the blade and adjusting the depth of cut

Holding the plane upside down, move the lateral adjustment lever so
that the cutting edge is level and centered in the mouth. To set the
cutting depth, turn the depth-of-cut adjustment knob so that the blade
protrudes from the mouth Usually about ¹⁄₆₄ inch is desirable *(above)*—
less for highly figured woods. Confirm the setting with a test cut on a
scrap board. The shavings should be paper-thin.

# BASIC TECHNIQUES

*Its blade adjusted to slice off the thinnest of shavings, a wooden smoothing plane evens out the surface of a workpiece.*

Hand planing procedures are the same regardless of what type or size of bench plane you use. Guide the tool along the surface by pushing it away from you with smooth, even strokes. (If you are using a Japanese plane, remember that it cuts on the pull, rather than the push, stroke.) Align your shoulder and hip with the plane, and grip the tool with both hands. Cup one hand around the front knob and keep the other at the back—either around the handle or the body.

Apply firm, constant pressure with every stroke. To keep the sole of the plane flat, exert more downward pressure on the front of the tool at the beginning of the stroke and shift the pressure to the rear as you approach the end. Your stock should always be clamped to a work surface.

It's important that you cut with the grain of the wood. You can usually determine the grain direction by running your hand along the board face or edge: The surface will feel smoother when your hand is moving with the grain and rougher when running against it. Another method is to make a test cut: The blade will chatter or catch on the wood when it is cutting against the grain.

# PLANING WITH THE WOOD GRAIN

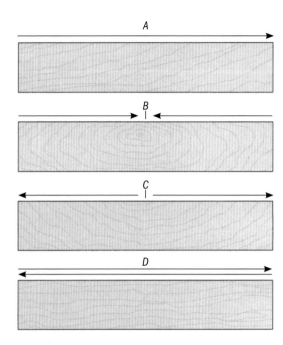

## Choosing the direction to plane

Determine the grain slope by inspecting the surface adjoining the one you are planing. The diagram at right shows several typical grain patterns with arrows indicating the best direction to plane. The direction may be constant from one end of a board to the other *(A)*. Or it may change, requiring that you plane the surface from each end toward the middle *(B)* or from the middle toward each end *(C)*. If the grain does not slope at all, you can plane the surface in a single pass from either end *(D)*. With irregular grain, guiding the plane at a slight angle to the direction of travel will help reduce the tearout by shearing the wood rather than tearing it. If you must plane against the grain, set the depth of cut to remove the thinnest possible shaving.

# PLANING A FACE

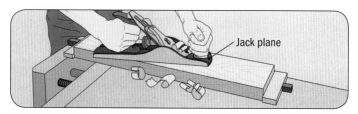

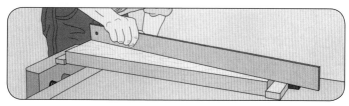

## Using a jack plane

Secure your stock face up on a work surface. Once you have oriented the plane with the wood grain, set the sole on the board with the blade just clear of one end. To remove stock quickly, plane with smooth, even strokes, angling the tool slightly to the grain *(above, top)*. To smooth the surface, keep the plane parallel to the grain, using a series of straight passes that slightly overlap. Examine the shavings as you work and adjust the cutting depth if you want a finer cut. Keep planing until the surface is smooth and shiny. To check whether the surface is flat, hold a straightedge across the face at several points *(above, bottom)*. The straightedge should rest flush against the surface. If there is a gap, plane the high spots and recheck.

**ShopTip**

**Checking or flatness with a bench plane**
If the sides of your plane are perfectly square to the sole, you can use it instead of a straightedge to determine whether a surface is flat. Simply tip the tool on edge and hold it on the surface at several points. If the plane rests flush along its entire length, the surface is flat.

# SMOOTHING EDGES

Jack plane

## Planing edges square

Secure the workpiece edge up in a vise. Guide a jack plane along the edge from one end of the board to the other, keeping the sole straight and flat on the surface *(above, top)*. To help steady the plane, you can press down on the toe with the thumb of your forward hand and curl your fingers around the face of the workpiece as you make the pass. If you need to plane the edges of several workpieces, secure them face to face in the vise, aligning their ends and edges. Then smooth their surfaces together *(above, bottom)* as you would a single board.

**ShopTip**

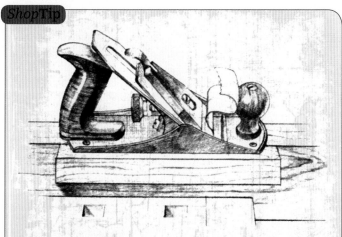

**A fence for planing edges**
To plane the edge of a workpiece square, attach a shop-made fence to the plane. Make the fence from ¼-inch-thick hardwood, cutting it to the same length as the sole of the plane. Fasten the fence to the plane using double-stick tape so that it overlaps the blade by about ¼ inch. Butt the fence against the face of a workpiece to keep the sole of the plane square on the edge as you make your pass.

# STRAIGHTENING OUT A LONG EDGE

Jointing plane

To plane the edge of a long workpiece, use a jointing plane. Its long sole makes it less likely than a jack plane to follow the contours that you want to remove. Secure the workpiece with the edge facing up; clamp one end to the workbench if necessary to keep the board steady. Starting at one end, guide the plane along the edge *(above)*, walking next to the workpiece until you reach the other end. Make as many passes as necessary until the plane slices off one long shaving from end to end.

# A BENCH STOP FOR PLANING

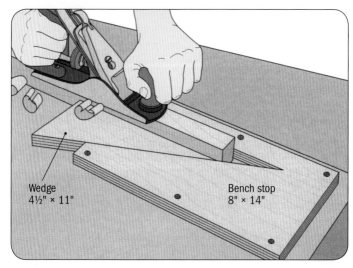

Wedge
4½" × 11"

Bench stop
8" × 14"

To secure a board to a work surface for planing without a vise or clamps, use the bench stop shown at left. Cut the stop from ¾-inch plywood to the dimensions suggested in the illustration, then saw a triangular wedge out of one end.

To use the stop, screw it to the work surface, then position your workpiece in the cut-out section, butting it against the straight side of the notch. Slide the wedge against the workpiece, tapping it with a wooden mallet to hold it snugly in place.

# PLANING END GRAIN

## Smoothing end grain

Use a bench plane or a block plane to smooth the ends of a workpiece. There are three ways to do the job without causing tearout at the end of each cut. Two are shown at right; a third method is shown on the facing page. Start by securing the workpiece end-up in a vise. For the first method, work toward the center, beginning at one edge of the board with the plane held at an angle to the sides. Guide the tool along the surface until the blade is about halfway across the end *(right, top)*, then repeat the process from the opposite edge. For the second method, cut a chamfer: Hold the

Block plane

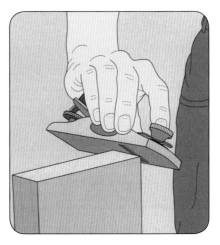

plane at an angle to flatten the corner *(right, bottom)*. Then make a pass along the entire end, beginning the stroke at the other edge.

Support block

## Using a support block

A third method of smoothing end grain allows you to make each pass with a single stroke. Secure the workpiece end up with support blocks clamped to both edges as shown. The blocks should be the same thickness as the workpiece; the one at the end of the pass should be level with the end to be planed. Guide the plane along the surface from one edge to the other, holding the tool at a slight angle to the sides of the board *(above)*.

# SALVAGING A BOWED BOARD

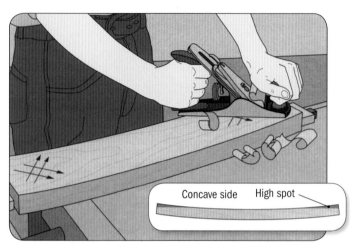

Concave side    High spot

## Planing a bowed board flat

Salvage a bowed board in two steps using a jack plane. First, secure the workpiece with its concave face up and shave away the high spots near the ends of the board *(inset).* Guide the plane at a 45° angle to the grain, alternating the direction of your strokes by 90°, as shown by the red arrows *(above).* Once the surface is

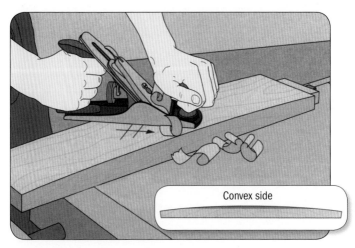

Convex side

flat, turn the workpiece over and repeat the process *(above)*. This time, you will be removing a single high spot in the middle of the board *(inset)*.

# TROUBLESHOOTING PLANING PROBLEMS

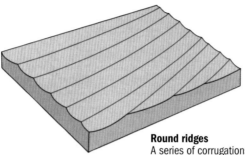

**Round ridges**
A series of corrugations results from using a plane with an excessively rounded or improperly ground cutting edge. To eliminate the ridges, square the end of the blade with a grinder *(page 10)*. (Rounding a blade and using it to remove stock rapidly from a rough surface is occasionally done deliberately; this technique is known as "hogging.")

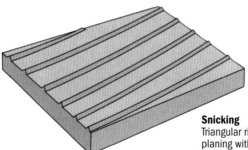

**Snicking**
Triangular ridges are caused by planing with a nicked or chipped cutting edge. Correct the problem by squaring the blade end with a grinder *(page 10)* and resharpening.

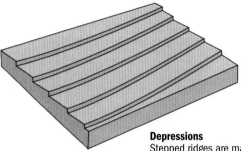

### Depressions

Stepped ridges are made by a cutting edge that is off-center in the mouth of the tool, making the blade protrude more from one side of the mouth than the other. If you observe these defects in your work, use the lateral adjustment lever to center the blade in the mouth of the plane.

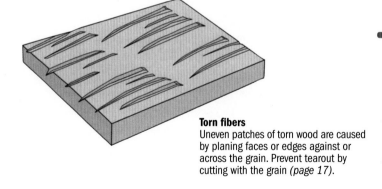

### Torn fibers

Uneven patches of torn wood are caused by planing faces or edges against or across the grain. Prevent tearout by cutting with the grain *(page 17)*.

# USING A BENCH RABBET PLANE

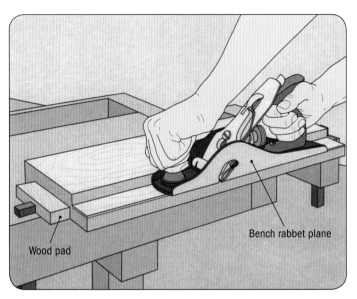

Bench rabbet plane

Wood pad

The bench rabbet plane has no built-in edge or depth guides so the width and depth of the rabbet are laid out with a marking gauge. This is not a bad idea even with planes that are equipped with a fence because it scores the grain and creates a crisp edge. After layout, nail or clamp a light strip of wood on the line denoting the rabbet's width. This guides the right edge of the plane for the length of the board. Once the cut is about ⅛" deep you can remove the improvised fence and plane to the gauge lines.

# RAISING A PANEL

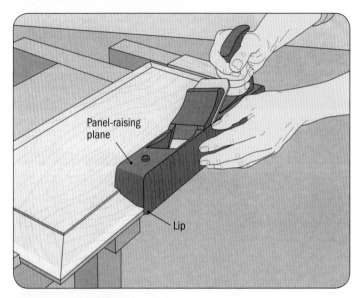

Panel-raising plane

Lip

## Planing the bevels

A panel-raising plane helps you bevel all four edges of a panel.
Cut the end grain first. Clamp the pan el on the workbench with its
edge extending off the table. Set the plan for a medium to fine cut and
make a few passes, guiding the plane along the surface with its lip flush
against the outer edge of the panel. Continue planing until the bevel
reaches full depth. Reposition the panel and bevel the opposite edge in
the same way. Then complete the long-grain edges, even though you're
likely to be planing against the grain on one side. Once in a while you
might find a matched pair of panel-raising planes—a right-hand model
and a left-hand one. This was supposed to allow you to cut with the
grain all around a panel, though in practice most workers had only one
plane and would have just accepted the need to go against the grain on
one side.

Raising a Panel

# CHAPTER 2

# Making Planes and Shooting Boxes

## SIMPLE SHOOTING BOX

This shooting box, or board (the terms are interchangeable), is extremely handy for working with thin stock. It makes square glue joints in thin stock a snap. Although the ramp is not necessary, it distributes blade wear a bit. Baltic birch plywood makes a stable base.

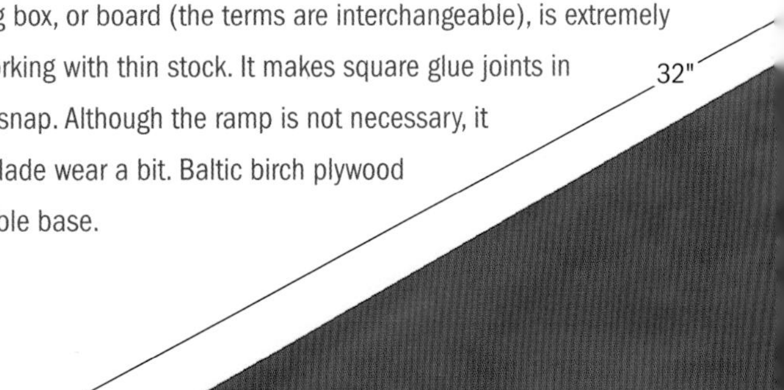

32"

12"

⅛"

©Ernie Conover 2010

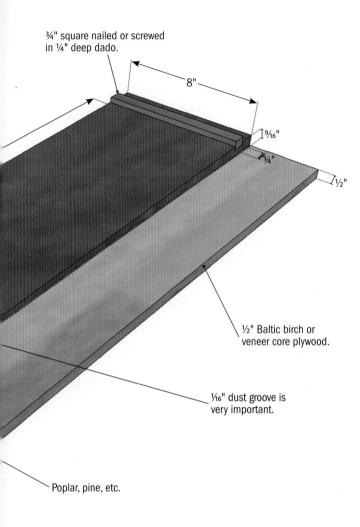

¾" square nailed or screwed in ¼" deep dado.

8"

⁹⁄₁₆"

¾"

½"

½" Baltic birch or veneer core plywood.

¹⁄₁₆" dust groove is very important.

Poplar, pine, etc.

# MITER SHOOTING BOX

Great for picture frames or any corner that has to be perfectly mitered.

Baltic birch plywood is a great material to make the base and riser from.

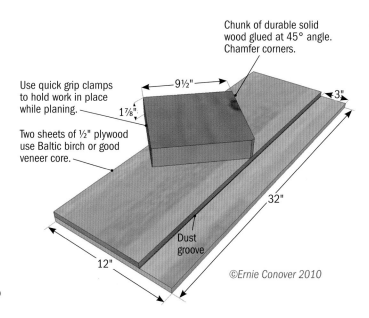

Chunk of durable solid wood glued at 45° angle. Chamfer corners.

Use quick grip clamps to hold work in place while planing.

Two sheets of ½" plywood use Baltic birch or good veneer core.

9½"

1⅞"

3"

32"

12"

Dust groove

©Ernie Conover 2010

# DONKEY'S EAR SHOOTING BOX

The name is derived from the fact that an end view looks like a donkey's ear. This shooting box is invaluable for mitering thin box lining material such as in jewelry cases. A table saw with a high-quality carbide blade makes short work of constructing this gem.

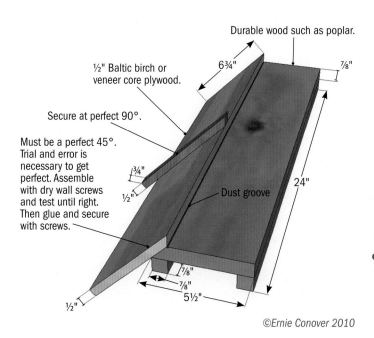

Durable wood such as poplar.

½" Baltic birch or veneer core plywood.

6¾"

⅞"

Secure at perfect 90°.

Must be a perfect 45°. Trial and error is necessary to get perfect. Assemble with dry wall screws and test until right. Then glue and secure with screws.

1¾"

½"

Dust groove

24"

⅞"

⅞"

5½"

½"

©Ernie Conover 2010

# A BENCH PLANE

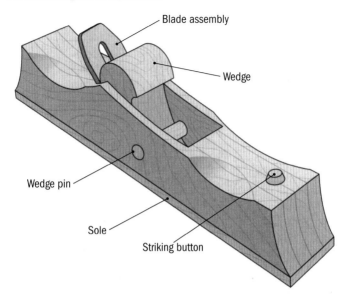

Blade assembly

Wedge

Wedge pin

Sole

Striking button

Although commercial steel bench planes look difficult to duplicate, you can build a wooden version in the shop that will cut as accurately as any store-bought tool. The parts list is straightforward: a hardwood block, a good plane blade and cap iron, and lengths of dowel.

The jointing plane shown at right was made using the "sandwich" method. First, a sole was glued on the bottom, then two cheeks were cut off the sides of the hardwood blank destined to become the plane body. The mortise for the blade and cap iron was sawn out next. Finally, the cheeks were glued back on to the body, and the blade and cap iron were put in place, held fast by a wooden wedge.

Start by cutting the blank for the body to size. Choose a dense, close-grained hardwood like maple or boxwood. If you cannot find a solid

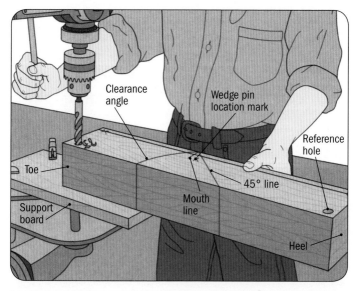

Labels in illustration: Clearance angle, Wedge pin location mark, Reference hole, Toe, 45° line, Mouth line, Support board, Heel

block of wood, glue up individual boards to the required dimensions (as was done for the illustrated plane). The size of the blank depends on the type of plane you wish to build. Smoothing planes are typically 7 to 9 inches long; jack planes range between 14 and 18 inches in length. The plane in the illustration is 18 inches long, but a jointing plane can be as long as 24 inches. Add 4 inches to the finished length you want. Make the blank 1½ inches wider than the blade. If you are building a smoothing plane, cut the blank 3 to 4 inches high; for a jack or jointing plane, make it 4 or 5 inches high.

Once the blank is cut to size, joint the bottom and glue on a sole. Use an oily and dense hardwood like cocobolo or lignum vitae for the sole, cutting it slightly longer and wider than the blank and

# A BENCH PLANE *(continued)*

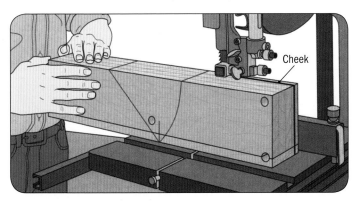

Cheek

at least ¼-inch thick. Attach the sole so that the uphill direction of the grain runs from the heel to the toe. Once the glue is dry, trim the excess wood from the sole and square the blank.

Next, mark out the blade mortise as shown on page 37. Mark a line across the sole for the mouth of the plane, placing it about one-third of the way from the toe. Then, from one end of this line, draw a line across one side of the blank at a 45° angle to the sole toward the heel. Then start another line from the same point, curving it gently toward the toe to form a clearance angle for the mortise. Transfer these lines across the top of the blank to the other side. Next, extend the mouth line up the sides 1¾ inches. Then measure horizontally ¾ inch back toward the heel and mark the center of the wedge pin. Finally, mark a location point for a reference dowel inside each corner of the blank. The marks should be close enough to the ends so that they can be cut off when the plane is trimmed to its finished size.

Place the blank on its side on a drill press table, clamping a support board underneath to prevent splintering when the bit exits the blank. Bore ½-inch-diameter holes at the corner marks *(page 37)* and a ¾-inch-diameter hole at the wedge pin location mark. Next,

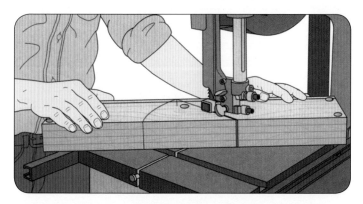

install a ¾-inch-wide resaw blade on the band saw and set up the rip fence on the table for a ½-inch-wide cut. Feed the blank into the blade with both hands to cut off one cheek, keeping the side flush against the fence and the sole flat on the table *(page 38)*. Repeat to cut a cheek from the other side of the blank, then set the cheeks aside.

Plane the sides of the blank until it is no more than ¹⁄₁₆ inch wider than the plane blade. Redraw the lines for the blade mortise on the sides of the blank, then install a ⅜-inch-wide blade on the band saw. Align the blade with one of the lines at the top of the blank, then feed the blank on its side into the blade using your right hand, while guiding it with your left hand *(above)*. Cut as close as possible to the point where the two marked lines meet but do not saw completely through the sole. Repeat to cut along the other line. Remove the waste piece and set it aside; later, you will fashion the piece into the blade wedge. Separate the blank into two pieces by hand and lightly sand the surfaces of the blade mortise.

To prepare the pieces for reassembly, test fit the cap iron and blade on the heel piece of the blank and mark the location of the cap

# A BENCH PLANE *(continued)*

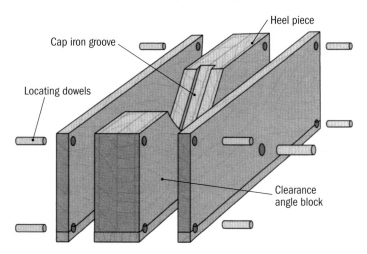

Heel piece

Cap iron groove

Locating dowels

Clearance angle block

iron screw. Then cut a groove for the screw *(above)*, stopping it 2 inches above the mouth of the plane. Glue the cheeks back onto the blank, inserting lengths of ½-inch-diameter dowel into the reference holes in the sides of the cheeks to help align the pieces accurately. Clamp the assembly together securely. Once the glue is dry, remove the clamps and cut off the doweled ends of the blank.

Next, prepare the wedge and wedge pin. Cut the wedge from the waste piece you sawed out of the blank. The bottom of the wedge should taper to a point, the surface that rests against the blade and cap iron should be flat, and the top should be rounded. For the wedge pin, cut a ¾-inch dowel to the same length as the width of the plane body. File a flat surface on one side of the pin large enough to accommodate the wedge.

Use the jointer to fine-tune the mouth opening of your plane. Set up the machine for a ⅟₃₂-inch depth of cut and make one pass. Then install the blade, cap iron, wedge, and wedge pin in the body and measure the distance from the cutting edge to the bottom of the sole. Your goal is a $\frac{1}{16}$-inch space, and several passes through the jointer–plane blade and wedge removed–may be necessary. Once the space is right, use a chisel to widen the mouth, shaving the front edge of the opening so that the blade just slips through it *(right, top)*. Check the mouth opening by installing the blade and wedge, and making a pass with the plane on a scrap board. If

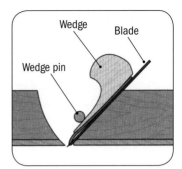

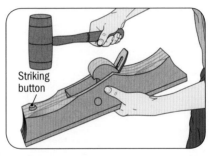

the shavings jam against the blade, rather than curling up over it, widen the mouth with the chisel.

Once the mouth is perfectly adjusted, you can modify the shape of the plane body to suit your hands. Finally, glue a striking button onto the top of the body near the toe. To loosen the wedge and remove the blade and cap iron from the tool, tap the striking button with a wooden mallet. To use the plane, set the blade and cap iron in position at the appropriate cutting depth, and install the wedge and its pin. Tap the wedge with a mallet, making sure it is holding the blade snugly in place.

*A Bench Plane*

# CHAPTER 3:
## Dating of Stanley-Bailey Bench Planes

**Quick reference** to Roger K. Smith classifications for dating the most common metal-body bench planes.

### Type 1    1867–1869 (Boston Bailey)

- Trademark stamped on iron and cap.

- Solid brass adjusting nut has right-hand thread.

- Solid lever cap with banjo-shaped spring.

- Higher and rounder sides and beaded edge at base of knob.

- No number cast on bed.

- Top corners of frog are rounded.

- No lateral adjustment lever.

- Round head screws on frog.

- Frog is shaped like letter *I*.

- High cross rib in casting in front of throat.

### Type 2    1869–1872

All features of Type 1 except:

- Early models of this type do not have Bailey's name on adjusting nut.

### Type 3    1872–1873 (major change)

All features of Type 2 except:

- New trademark on irons.

- Hump in sides moved farther back on casting.

- Special frog piece attached to a vertical rib between sides.

- Adjusting nut recessed.

- Lever cap has recessed back.

- Fillets removed form cross rib ahead of the throat and rib lowered.

- Change in handle design.

## Type 4    1874–1884
## (major change)

All features of Type 3 except:

- Now equipped with the standard full size frog as in Type 2 and tip of Y adjusting lever now square.

- Frog receiver enlarged but still milled smooth.

- Flat head cap screws now used to hold frog.

## Type 5    1885–1888
## (major change)

All features of Type 4 except:

- New trademark on irons in later specimens of this type.

- Plane numbers now cast on toe in front of knob.

- Top corners of frog no longer rounded.

- First lateral adjuster with two patent dates stamped 2-8-76 and 10-21-84.

## Type 6    1888–1890

All features of Type 5 except:

- Anti-friction disc added to regulator. (Patent dated 2-8-76, 10-21-84 and 7-24-88.)

*In 1885 the lateral adjuster was introduced to facilitate accurate side-to-side adjustment of the cutter. In 1888 the "anti-friction disk" was added. Both features were patented. The regulator on this transition plane has both patents, meaning it was made within 20 years of the earlier date.*

- Frog receiver now has two grooves cast across top in line with frog screws.

- Bead eliminated at base of knob.

- Change in handle design.

## Type 6a    1891–1892

All features of Type 6 except:

- New trademark on iron of models manufactured in 1892.

## Type 7   Stanley 1893–1899

All features of Type 6a except:

- Bailey's name and patent dates eliminated from adjusting nut and cap iron.

- Stud for adjusting nut are threaded left-handed, which makes adjustment normal to Western thinking.

- 1892 patent date on irons (if original).

- Spacing of number markings now 1 inch.

- S casting mark of foundry who made casting.

## Type 8   1899–1902

All features of Type 7 except:

- S mark eliminated from casting.

- Only one patent date on regulator: 7-24-88.

- B casting mark on most specimens.

## Type 9   1902–1907 (major change)

All features of Type 8 except:

- B mark in casting eliminated.

- Bailey's name now cast on toe.

- Major frog improvement. New style frog and frog receiver that keeps frog square to body. (Patent dated 3-25-02 and 8-19-02.)

## Type 10   1907–1909

All features of Type 9 except:

- Center rib of frog receiver enlarged and arched and captive head adjusting screw added.

- New trademark on irons starting in 1907 (Stanley Rule & Level Co. New Britain, Conn., U.S.A., in four lines with Stanley arched).

- Change in handle design.

## Type 11   1910–1918

All features of Type 10 except:

- Patent date 4-19-10 added in back of frog.

- New trademark stamped on iron with Type 9 information arranged in a V shape.

## Type 12   1919–1924 (major change)

All features of Type 11 except:

- High knob introduced.

- Adjusting knob increased in sized to 1¼" in diameter.

*Between 1902 and 1907 the frog was greatly improved. The #2 at the right has the original design which required the user to bring the frog square to the mouth by eye. At left is the improved design with a rig in the casting and a groove in the frog so that it always stays square to the mouth. Between 1907 and 1909 the captive head screw in the body was added, with the mating tab on the frog. This allows micrometer adjustment of the throat opening.*

- Lever cap edges not as rounded and less radius to lever.

- New trademark stamped on iron in 1920 (Stanley Sweet Heart with New Britain, Conn., U.S.A.).

- New trademark stamped on iron in 1921 and 1922 (Stanley Sweet Heart with Made in U.S.A.).

- New trademark stamped on iron in 1923 to 1935 (Stanley Sweet Heart logo slightly larger).

## Type 13   1925–1928

All features of Type 12 except:

- 4-19-10 patent date behind frog.

- Rectangular Stanley logo cast in lever cap.

## Type 14   1929–1930

All features of Type 13 except:

- MADE IN U.S.A. now added in front of knob.

- Raised ring around knob to prevent splitting.

*Between 1919 and 1924 the higher knob on left was introduced which gave the user better purchase. Knobs are not a good indicator of date because they were often replaced. They can reinforce a dating, however.*

## Type 15    1931–1932

All features of Type 14 except:

- MADE IN U.S.A. now cast behind frog.

- Patent date marking behind frog eliminated.

## Type 16    1933–1941 (major change)

All features of Type 15 except:

- Kidney-shaped hole in lever cap, which is now nickel plated along with screw that secures lever cap and the frog adjusting screw.

- New trademark on iron (Stanley Sweet Heart logo still larger).

- Raised rib in casting at toe.

## Type 17    1942–1947 (war production)

All features of Type 16 except:

- Handles and knobs are of hardwood with dark rosewood stain.

- Body casting noticeably heavier with thicker sides.

- Adjusting nut may be a smaller diameter and of steel or of a larger diameter with hard rubber ring around steel.

- Some specimens may have no frog adjusting screw or kidney hole in lever cap.

*Although lever caps get switched around, they are an indicator of date. Left to right: Cap prior to 1925; middle cap with embossed logo was introduced between 1925 and 1928; right cap with orange enamel was introduced between 1933 and 1941. The kidney-shaped hole, an improvement on the earlier tear-drop shape, was a patented feature. Nickel plating was also introduced about the same time.*

### Type 18    1946–1947

All features of Type 17 except:

- Handles of a new design and painted black.

- Large brass adjusting knob now with diamond knurling.

- Body casting now lighter in weight as in prewar production.

### Type 19    1948–1961

All features of Type 18 except:

- Frog receiver design changed to provide an arched buttress.

- Rosewood handles reintroduced in 1949 have a thick varnish nearly obscuring the wood grain.

- STANLEY letters on regulator lever now reads vertically.

- Brass adjusting nuts back to straight knurling.

- Late models (1958–61) have hardwood handles with dark stain.

### Type 20    1962–1967

All features of Type 19 except:

- Castings now painted blue.

- Handles have light colored stain.

- Forked adjusting lever now two stamped pieces.

- Regulator lever now bent for thumb grip rather than separate piece and vertical STANLEY eliminated.

*Quick Reference*

# THE *Missing* SHOP MANUAL SERIES

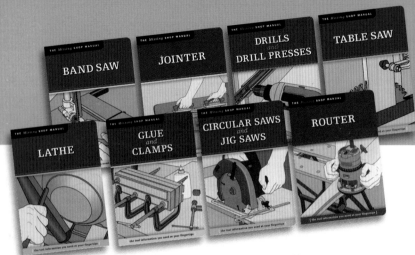